Life Is Like A Journey On A Train

What Is Life

Dr. CA Vishnu Bharath Alampali

PARTRIDGE
A Penguin Random House Company

ISBN:	Hardcover	978-1-4828-4438-2
	Softcover	978-1-4828-4439-9
	eBook	978-1-4828-4437-5

To order additional copies of this book, contact
Partridge India
000 800 10062 62
orders.india@partridgepublishing.com

www.partridgepublishing.com/india

Contents

Preface

I am indeed glad to publish my 19th book under the title "LIFE IS LIKE A JOURNEY ON A TRAIN" Life is very precious & special, no one has yet realised why and what for life. Life is half spent before we can even understand what it is. Life is sweet for those who think and life is bitter for those who feel. Life is worth living, people are worth loving and God is worth trusting. Life can only be understood backwards. Life is made of millions of moments. You only live once, make the best use of it. What matters is not how long you live but how well you live. When life is like a sour lemon, make the best use of it; make lemonade. When a great thinker was asked- what is the meaning of life? He replied- life itself has "No" meaning, but life is an opportunity to create a meaning. The external cycle of Life rolls on uninterrupted… Jubilation in victory and tribulation in defeat.. Celebration in success and regret in failure... Happiness in union and sadness in separation…. Life continues on its predestined path from time immemorial to time everlasting. So predictable…. so normal… so ordinary, and yet so very unique….so beautifully magical… so unbelievably miraculous.

I have narrated in a capsule form and you have to read, think and register in your mind and only then it could be digested. Life is from the date of birth to date of death and how you utilize the precious life is entirely left to your discretion. As you cannot carry anything with you, when you depart from this world, the good work done will be there forever to benefit humanity.

Family (Father And Mother I Love You) by chance you get your family, very limited in number and you do not have any choice of what so ever nature to choose. Friend –(The person who freak till end is the friend) could be by choice and it is up to you to choose, unlike relatives & Family there is no limit to have friends. If you have good family and friends, your life is supposed to be interesting, enjoyable and brings immense happiness.

"Life is not an ipod to listen to your favorite songs. It is a radio, you must adjust yourself to every frequency and enjoy whatever comes in it."

If you want to know the power of God, see the Sun. If you want to know the beauty of God, see the Moon and if you want to know the best creation of God, see the Mirror. What you see in mirror is yourself that is best creation of God. Have thrust in yourself and make best use of Precious Life.

Dr. CA Vishnu Bharath AS.

Life Is Like A Journey On A Train

"*Life is not an iPod to listen to your favorite songs. It is a radio; you must adjust yourself to every frequency and enjoy whatever comes in it. Life is almost like a journey on a train, all of us are tourists & God is our travel agent who has already fixed all our routes, reservations & destinations, So! Trust him & enjoy the trip called Life. Life is between date of birth to date of death and no one knows when the end comes. You are born crying and when you depart the others will cry, one has to make an impact during the life time. One should leave behind beautiful memories, for those who will continue to travel on the train of life. I wish everyone a very happy & joyful journey of Life and be thankful to God for such a lovely trip and more importantly thank you for being one of the passenger on my train!*

The Train journey starts from a station, carries on with different tracks, route, stations, every one hopes the journey to be safe, study and timely but sometimes it so happens with minor accidents, sometimes may be major accidents but the journey goes on and on....By birth one has parents may be also siblings who take care so protectively, you think life is full of roses and you will get what you wanted, the wants as a child are very limited to the extent of some food and entertainment but as you grow the wants enhance imp proportionately, many people come in your way may be the relatives, friends, well-wishers, enemies and many others. You do not know when and which station your parents depart, your siblings depart and when you yourself depart, as birth is certain the death is also certain but no one knows when, how and where. The interesting thing is one by one depart from your life and one by one join your life as it happens on a train journey. You are bound to get your spouse and then family of your own. The God has made Life so interesting for those who think and bitter for those who feel. Nnature is a gift of God, one has to live with nature and you get everything in plenty what is basically required for comfortable living, that is air, water, clothing, shelter and food.

Among all living beings, human life is most precious and enjoy the innumerable benefits that other living beings don't have, compare to any living being, human is most superior and wants of human are un limited unlike the other living beings. It is entirely in your hands how you carry on the journey of life, either by making the journey a pleasant one, joy, fantasy, enjoyable, adorable, interesting, beautiful, goodbye's, farewells etc., or by making boring, disturbing, sorrowful, painful, not only to yourself but also for the people who travel along with you." One thing you should make sure that when you depart, you should leave behind beautiful memories for those who will continue to travel on the train of life. I sincerely hope and wish everyone a joyful journey, specially the reader of my book.

Life is only traveled once: Today's moment becomes tomorrow's memory. Enjoy every moment good or bad because the gift of life is life itself.

*   Simple living –high thinking is the best way to live.
*   Life is not measured by the time span we live, but by the quality built into it.
*   Be in harmony with life and nature will bless you thousand fold.
*   Life is a tragedy for those who feel, and comedy for those who think.
*   The remembrance of a well-spent life makes life sweet.
*   From what you get, we can make a living; what we give, however makes a life.
*   High living and low thinking degrades human values.
*   If you can smile at life, life will always smile at you.

* Enjoy your own life without comparing it with that of another.
* Life can only be understood backwards but it must be lived forwards.
* Never get so busy making a living that you forget to make a life.
* The tragedy of life is what dies inside the man while he lives.
* There are three ingredients to the good life; learning, earning, and yearning.
* Value your life and others will also value you.
* We live as though we will never die, then die as though we never lived.
* Life is not to be feared, it is only to be understood.
  * The softness of a person's nature does not mean weakness. Water is softer, but its force can break the strongest rocks.
  * One has to take care of his actions because they will become his habits. One has to take care of his habits because they will form his character.
  * Make your anger so expensive that no one can get it easily and make your happiness so cheap that everyone gets it from you.
  * Lucky people get opportunities, brave people create opportunities, but real winners are those who convert their problems into opportunities.
  * Money in the hands of a bad human being will destroy the existing world. Money in the hands of a good human being will create a new world.
  * Some succeed because they are destined to, but most succeed because they are determined to.

* Victory is not a property of brilliants but it is a crown for those who pursue hard work with confidence and devotion.

* Silence on lips may avoid many problems. But, speaking with open heart can solve most of the problems. Always speak with the open heart.

* A happy person is always happy not because everything is right in their life. They are happy because their attitude towards everything is right.

* Never worry for the delay in your success as compared to others. Because construction of wonders takes more time, than ordinary structures.

* Don't turn back half way from your goal, as the distance still remains the same, either ways. The most desperate time in life is not when you are sad. It's when you have lots to say and you don't find that special one to hear you.

* Success is never permanent. Failure is never final. So always, do not stop putting efforts until your victory makes a history.

* Forget your own sadness by creating a little happiness for others. Because when you are good to others, you are best to yourself.

* Entire water of the sea can't sink a ship unless it gets inside the ship. Similarly negativity of the world can't put you down unless you allow it to get inside YOU.

* You will never reach your destination if you stop and throw stones at every dog that barks.

* Success of relationship does not depend on how good understanding we have but it depends upon how we avoid misunderstanding.

* Life survives on changes. Instead of avoiding, take every change as a challenge. It will either give us success or it will teach us how to succeed.

* The ups and down in life are very important to keep us going because a straight line even in an ECG means we are not alive.

* Life is the most difficult exam. Many people fail because they try to copy others - not realising that everyone has a different question paper.

* Think of "LIFE", certain you will find yourself charged! Think of "NATURE" certain you will find yourself charged.

* Don't think that time will change our life. Time only changes the expiry dates of the opportunities.

* Motivation accelerates your journey to Success while Consistency will drop you at the destination. Both are vital things to accomplish on your Journey to Success.

* What is BLESSED is sure to happen, accept what comes in with mind kept open!
  What is BLOCKED will not at all happen worry not and enjoy with life kept open.

* The price of discipline is always less than the pain of regret. Self-discipline is the biggest investment for success in life.

* The correct temperature at home is maintained by warm hearts and cool heads, not by good ventilation, fans and air conditioners.

* No and yes are words that need thought. Many of the troubles in life are the result of saying yes too soon or no too late.

* Open your book of life only to a few people because in this world very few care to understand the chapters others are just curious to know the story.

When you move your focus from competition to contribution, life becomes celebration. Never try to defeat people, just win them.

* You cannot change your future. But, you can change your habits, and surely your habits will change your future.

* "No moment is permanent in life" read this line whenever you are happy, angry, upset, cheated, lonely or sad. It works always.

* If you desire to blossom like a rose in the garden, you have to learn the art of adjusting with the thorns.

* Always look for what is wrong before looking who is wrong. This helps to keep your relations good and strong.

* A blind person asked God, can there be anything worse than losing eye sight? He replied, yes, losing your vision.

* Best philosophy in life is to keep the mind happy, I do not know if success gives happiness but l know that a happy mind can lead to success.

* It's a fact when you are happy; you want to reach the person you love most. But when you are sad, you want to reach the person who loves you most.

One of the greatest victories you can gain over someone is to beat him at politeness.

* **Do not lower your goals to the height of your abilities. Instead, heighten your abilities to the level of your goals.**

* **"A happy person is always happy not because everything is right in their life.**
  They are happy because their attitude towards everything is right".

* **To be Kind is more important than to be right. Many times what people need is not a brilliant mind that speaks but a special heart that listens.**

* Do not have fear and step back from battle field but be victorious.

What Is Life?

- You want and you get that is luck, you want and you wait that is time, you want and you earn that is ability, you want but you compromise and that is life.
- No one has travelled the road of success, without crossing streets of failure. God never promised easy journeys in life. He only promised Great Destinations.
- A lot of people end up unhappy in life only because they usually make the mistake of taking Permanent decision, on temporary emotions.
- Never forget three types of people in your LIFE:
  (1) Who helped you in your difficult times?
  (2) Who left you in your difficulties and
  (3) Who put you in difficult times?
- Fantastic lines of Mother Teresa" "if you're EYES are positive, you will like the world. If your TONGUE is positive the world will like you".
- Success and Excuses do not talk to each other. So if we give Excuses forget about Success and if we want Success, forget about Excuses.
- BELL has NO SOUND until someone rings it. SONG has NO TUNE, until someone sings it. Never hide your FEELINGS because it has no value till someone feel it.

- Why there is so much stress in life? It is because we focus too much on improving our LIFESTYLE rather than our LIFE.
- The most difficult phase of life is not when no one understands you; But, It is when you don't understand yourself.
- For everything you have missed, you have gained something else; and for everything you gain, you lose something else.
- It is about your outlook towards life. You can either regret or rejoice, choice is yours.
- It feels good to stand on ground and watch up high at your AIM…. But it feels BEST, when you stand up high and others watch YOU as their AIM.
- Life is similar to Boxing game. Defeat is NOT declared when you fall down. It is declared when you refuse to get Up.
- The best pair in the world is "Smile and Cry". They will not meet each other at a time. If they meet, that is the best moment of the life…….!
- When a cyclone strikes… Huge trees get uprooted, but the simple grass survives. Be noble and humble like the grass. Simple but strong.
- Life is not about the people who act true in your presence. It is about the people who remain true in your absence. Keep them safe in your Heart.
- One thing we need to learn from life is that getting 'UPSET' will not help. Instead getting 'UP' to 'SET' the things right will Help.
- Success in life will create crowd behind you.

- Loneliness in life will create space around you. But tough times in Life will create the true person in YOU.
- Our HOPE should be like our HAIR AND NAILS. No matter how many times they get CUT. They never STOP GROWING.
- If the Road is beautiful then, worry about the destination, but if the destination is beautiful, then don't worry about the road.
- When you are in ANGER, you are just 1 letter short in DANGER. While you are GOOD to others, you are 1 letter more than GOD.
- Life never seems to be the way we want it, but we live it the best way we can. There is no perfect life, but we can fill it with perfect moments.
- Never hold your head high with pride and ego, even the winner of a Gold Medal gets his medal only when he bows his head down.
- Life is like a Badminton Match. If you want to win Serve Well and Return well and do remember that the game starts with LOVE ALL.
- Everyone wants HAPPINESS. No one wants PAIN. But you can't have a RAINBOW without a LITTLE RAIN.
- God is always playing chess with us. He makes moves in our life and then see how we react to the challenge, so keep on making the best move before it is check mate.
- Reach boldly for the miracle. God knows your gifts, your hindrances, and the condition you are in at every moment.

- Family, Health, Friends and Spirit : These things do not come with price tag, but when we lose them, we realise the cost.
- We are very good Lawyers for our mistakes. Very good Judges for others mistakes.
- EYES express FEELINGS better than words TOUCH shows CARE more than words but WORDS when properly used can catch the EYES and TOUCH the heart.
- Never try to maintain Relations in your Life. Just try to maintain life in your relations.
- Worries are like Moon. One day will increase, one day will decrease, other day may not be seen, so don't worry for anything always be cool.
- Our life begins with our CRY, Our life ends with others CRY, Try to utilise this gap with laugh as much as possible in between these cries.
- Hardest moment is not when you lose something & tears come out of your eyes, but it's when you lose something and still manage to smile.
- How beautifully GOD keeps on adding one more day in our life!! Not only because you need it...because someone else need you every day.
- A Good Relation does not depend on how good Understanding we have... But it depends on how we avoid Misunderstanding.
- We categories experiences as Success or Failure, Good or Bad, Positive or Negative, Favorable or Unfavorable, This or That.... but in reality, experiences have no negative connotation. Every experience simply offers you learning.

- If you are Depressed or if you are Confused or if you are Hurt then don't worry. Go in front of the mirror, YOU will find the best person who will solve all your problems.
- A "Broken Trust" can be best described as Melted Chocolate. No matter how hard you try to freeze it, it will never return in its true shape.
- To become learned, each day add something. To become enlightened, each day drop something. Never feel bad if people remember you only at the time of their need.
- Feel privileged that they think of you like a candle in the darkness of their life.
- There are many things in life that will catch your eye, but only a few will catch your heart…. Pursue those.
- The single finger which wipes out tears during our failure is much better than the ten fingers which comes together to clap for our victory.
- "if your EYES are positive, you will like the world. If your TONGUE is positive, the world will like you".
- Be what you want to be not what others want to see. – Never try to impress others. If you start trying impressing on others, you will fail. (you're cheating not only yourself but also the persons whom you're trying to impress).
- Life is to live, not to act.
- To be happy in life, you must learn the difference between what you want vs need.
- When you are successful, your well-wishers know who you are. When you are unsuccessful, you know who your well-wishers are.

- Life is not measured by the breaths we take but by the moments that take our breath away.
- It is great confidence in a friend to tell him your faults; greater is to tell his/hers.
- Most courageous person is the one who accepts his/her mistakes & weakness.
- Effort is important, but knowing where to make an effort in your life, makes all the difference.
- Never take some one for granted, Hold every person Close to your Heart because you might wake up one day and realize that you have lost a diamond while you were too busy collecting stones." Remember this always in life.
- Some people think that to be strong is to never feel pain. In Reality the strong people are the ones who feel it, understand it, and accept it.
- My pain may be the reason for somebody's laugh. But my laugh should never be the reason for somebody's pain. Never expect things to happen. Struggle and make them to happen.
- Never expect yourself to be given a good value. Create a value of your own.

- Don't handicap your children by making their lives easy.
- It is so funny that in the past nobody had watch but they had plenty of Time, on the contrary everybody has watch now but nobody has any time.
- A chain is only as strong as its weakest link" and this is very true to every aspect of our life.
- No matter how many good habits we practice, one negative habit can damage everything.
- No matter how good our decisions have been in life, one wrong decision will change the entire flow after that.
- No matter how strong a family is, one member's action might disturb the peace and happiness of the entire family.
- Give a man a fish and he will eat for a day and look for other person to give him fish. Teach him how to fish, and he will not only eat fish but also give to others.
- True Love is eternal; cherish the Love when you have got the chance, For once it leaves you, and it would be difficult to get it back. Don't let Love be only a memory to you.

- Yes and No are very powerful words, Mean them when you say them and Respect them when you hear them.
- No dreamer is ever too small & No dream is ever too big. The future belongs to those who dare to dream and are ready to work for it.
- Little keys open BIG Locks, Simple words reflect GREAT Thoughts. Your smile can cure HEART Blocks, So keep on smiling it ROCKS!
- There are only two choices. Either you can be a history reader or become a history maker.
- "Half of the problems in life are because we ACT without THINKING and rest half is because we keep THINKING without ACTING"
- Every little smile can touch somebody's heart. No one is born happy but all of us are born with the ability to create happiness.
- Character is like Tree and Reputation is like its Shadow. The Shadow is what we think of it; the Tree is the real thing.
- If a drop of water falls on Lake, it loses its Identity, If it falls on Lotus it Shines, If it falls on Shell it becomes a Pearl, drop is the same but Company matters.
- The quality of a man's life is in direct proportion to his commitment to excellence, regardless of his chosen field of endeavor.
- YES & NO are too short words which need a long thought. Most of the things we miss in life are because of saying 'No' too early and 'YES' too late.
- All our dreams cannot be translated into reality, but they can act as foundation stone for glorious future, be positive always.

- Be close with someone who makes you happy but be closer with someone who can't be happy without you. Feel the difference!!

- A tongue has no bones, but it can break a heart and also it can be a pillar of Strength to a broken heart.

- One good deed a day works in life like a thread woven each day in the quilt that will keep you warm in winters.

- Life is not a sharp knife to cut all those bad memories. But life is a needle to weave golden thread of sweet memories.

- Being good is not very easy; it's like being a goal keeper. No matter how many goals you save, people remember only the one you missed. That's life.

- Only a few people come into your life as blessings, whereas all others come into your life as lessons, cherish the blessings and value the lessons

    (1) The price of discipline is always less than the pain of regret; self- discipline is the biggest investment for success in life.

    (2) We cannot tailor-make the situations in life, we can tailor-make the attitude to face those situations.

    (3) Mistake is a single page of life but relation is a complete book, so do not lose a full book for single page.

- Richest wealth is wisdom, strongest weapon is patience, best security is faith, most effective tonic is laughter and surprisingly all are free.

- Always take extra care of three things in life, which are trust, promise and relationship because they do not make noise when they break, they only create silence.

Leave Your Ego –
You Are A Small Creature

One who has everything, i.e., power, authority, money, etc., is bound to acquire ego and thinks that he can do what he likes, and he is the master. He is intoxicated by his wealth. As he has authority, he is arrogant, and he thinks he is superman and he is above all. In the vast and wonderful universe, there are countless beings, the sky, the sun, the moon, innumerable planets, stars and in front of all this, what is he? He is a small creature in this universe. If every need is provided, it is due to the mercy of Lord and he expects you to do good to humanity and your fellow beings. In the matter of a second He can snatch everything away from you. If one is egoistic, it is due to his ignorance or inadequate knowledge. As long as he has authority, he can abuse this authority in his personal interest but when he loses authority; his conscious pricks and he will have no peace of mind and has to undergo sleepless nights. One has to judiciously use what the Lord has given and he is answerable to the Lord one day.

The sense of responsibility is the only force that can keep a man under restraint. If a person is convinced that there is nobody to call him to account, no matter what he demands, and that there is no power above him that can punish him, he will naturally tend to lose all sense of discipline and lead an irresponsible and in disciplined life. And this is true of the family, the nation, and of mankind at large.

Life

There is a saying, that one should have British type of house, American type of Business, Chinese type of food, Japanese type of Wife and Jewish type of Intelligence, Indian type of Climate to enjoy the Life, but in reality the Lord gives you what you deserve and one should be happy with what you have and enjoy the Life. The creator of every human being gives happiness & sorrow in the measure what he deserves as per his karma, just like the lock is not made without key, problems are not given without solutions, one has to have patience to overcome and make his life easy and ongoing. One does not know the purpose of his arrival to this world, till his death. If one understand that he/she is mini creature in this universe and take life as it comes, he is the most successful and happy person. The best example, we can have is the most popular President of United States of America, Mr. Abraham Lincoln, who lost his mother at the age of 14, his wife at the age of 21, his son at the age of 24, he had Nervous breakdown twice, he lost his Vice President ship at the age of 48 and become the most successful President of United States at the age of 51 years and proved to the world that one should not lose confidence and the situations and circumstances makes him more stronger, confident, determined and what not.

Everyone takes life for granted: no one realise how precious life is! One has to think in a relaxed state of mind, peaceful atmosphere and look around him and also compare with other living beings to realize how precious human life is! Only on realization, one will enjoy every moment without wasting precious life. Yesterday is past and tomorrow is future; we normally are worrying about the past and thinking about the future and forget the day which is before us that is so precious. It is well said that everything happens with the grace of God, but effort should be put forth and the result can be left to the Almighty. In life, failure is not the real end, but it can be the real beginning of success, yesterday is an experience, today is an experiment, and Tomorrow is an expectation. One should use his experience in his experiment to achieve his expectation.

There are lots of beautiful things around us. It's just a matter of how we see it and whether we're able to realize it. In life, of course there are always some ups and downs. However, I believe, that even in the most difficult situation, there's always a beautiful thing. As wise people say, "Everything happens for a reason."

Life has no Pause Button
Dreams have no Expiry Date
Time takes no Holiday
We should adopt these principles

Life Is Very Precious

- All living things are made up of cells. The simplest organism consists of one cell and human is made of billions of cells. To those who see life with loving eyes, Life is beautiful. To those who speak with tender care, Life is peaceful. To those who help with gentle hands, Life is full and those who care with compassionate hearts, Life is beyond measure. Life is so very precious and every day is a gift, make every minute meaningful and enjoy the best. Look at the Sun, Moon, Stars, Rivers, Ocean, Mountain, Plant, Tree, Animals, Birds etc., enjoy the creation, all are given to you by Almighty to have peaceful & enjoyable life.

- LIFE is the sequence of physical and mental experiences that make up the existence of an individual. Life is conscious existence. Life is the manner of living from birth to death.

- Life is half spent before we can even understand what it is. Life is sweet for those who think:, life is bitter for those who feel.

- Life is not in the living but in the liking. Life would be too smooth if it had no rubs in it. Where there is life, there is hope. Whatever you give to life, it gives you back.

- How you die is quite important, but far more important is how you live. If we live truly, we shall see truly.

- If your life is worth living, it is worth recording. Life is 10% what happens to us and 90% how we react to it. Life in abundance comes only through great love.
- Life is like a race between a cat and a rat. Rats mostly win because rats run for their life whereas cats run for their food.
- Life is raw material; it is in our hands, and we can shape it as we want. Life is a tragedy for those who feel and a comedy for those who think.
- Life is worth living, people are worth loving and God is worth trusting. Life can only be understood backwards.
- You can't change the past but you can look forward to the future. Only you can change your life; no one else can do it for you.
- The best way to prepare for life is to begin to live. The state of your life is nothing more than a reflection of your state of mind. The quality, not the longevity, of one's life is what is important.
- Death is not the greatest loss in life. The greatest loss is what dies inside us while we are still alive. Live before you die.
- Life is made of millions of moments. You only live once, make the best use of it. What matters is not how long you live but how well you live.

- Remember: you were born to live, don't just live because you were born. Accept responsibility for your life.
- When you were born you cried and the world rejoiced. Live your life in such a manner that when you die, the world cries and you rejoice.
- The most difficult phase of life is not when no one understands you; it is when you don't understand yourself.
- No one grows old by living, only by losing interest in living.
- When life is like a sour lemon, make the best use of it; make lemonade.
- We make a living by what we get, but we make a life by what we give.

Basic Features Of Life

Nobody can go back and start a new life.

The longer I live the more I realize.

Dream as if you live forever but live as if you die today.

Love as much as you breathe and love as much as you live.

Life is full of beauty, live your life to the fullest potential.

One day your life will flash before your eyes, make sure it is worth watching.

It's only when we truly know and understand that we have a limited time on earth -- and that we have no way of knowing when our time is up -- that we will begin to live each day to the fullest, as if it is the only one we have.

A life lived in love will never be dull.

One must work and dare if one really wants to live.

Life is meaningless only if we allow it to be. Each of us has the power to give life meaning, to make our time and our bodies and our words into instruments of love and hope.

Live every act fully, as if it were your last.

Without some goal and some effort to reach it, no one can live.

Respect for the fragility and importance of every individual life is the mark of an educated man.

I don't want to get to the end of my life and find that I lived just the length of it. I want to have lived the width of it as well.

Let us endeavor so to live that when we come to die even the undertaker will be sorry.

Life has got to be lived -- that's all there is to it.

Life is not measured by the breaths you take, but by its breathtaking moments.

Life is what you make of it. Always has been, always will be.

You have to pay the price. You will find that everything in life exacts a price, and you will have to decide whether the price is worth the prize.

Most people can look back over the years and identify a time and place at which their lives changed significantly. Whether by accident or design, these are the moments when, because of a readiness within us and collaboration with events occurring around us, we are forced to seriously reappraise ourselves and the conditions under which we live and to make certain choices that will affect the rest of our lives.

Life's challenges are not supposed to paralyze you; they're supposed to help you discover who you are.

How far you go in life depends on your being tender with the young, compassionate with the aged, sympathetic with the striving, and tolerant of the weak and strong because some time in life you would have been all of these.

Love life and life will love you back. Love people and they will love you back.

That it will never come again is what makes life so sweet. Life is short, but there is always time enough for courtesy.

The principle of life is that life responds by corresponding; your life becomes the thing you have decided it shall be.

**Night Is shorter than day for those who dream,
But, the Day is shorter than Night for those who make their dreams come True**

Balance Sheet Of Life

Yesterday is a stale cheque, tomorrow is postdated cheque and today is hard currency, enjoy every moment.

Never blame a day in your life:

Good days give happiness,

Bad days give experience,

Worst days give you a lesson and

Best day gives you memories

Imagine there is a bank that credits your account each morning with 86,400. It carries over no balance from day to day. Every evening it deletes whatever part of the balance you failed to use during the day. What would you do? Draw out every cent, of course! Have a perfect Balance Sheet of Life:

IT IS TIME

Time is
Too slow for those who wait,
Too swift for those who fear,
Too long for those who grieve,
Too short for those who rejoice
But for those who love..............
Time is Eternity.

This is the beginning of a new day. You have been given this day to use as you wish. You can waste it or use it for good. What you do today is important because you are exchanging a day of your life for it. When tomorrow comes, this day will be gone forever; in its place is something that you have left behind...let it be something good."

The interesting fact is that God gives birth to millions of living things, but every one of these is different from the other in looks and complexion, in voice, and disposition, in powers and faculties, in qualities and moral caliber. Even brothers born to the same father and mother are never identical to each other. When even identical twins are not alike, imagine how great the caliber of our creator is!

A study on 500 lives who are successful and wealthy people reveals that there was one great characteristic that separated the successful from the unsuccessful ones is the habit of taking quick decisions and rarely changing them as opposed to taking slow decisions and changing them quickly.

A life without an AIM is like an Envelope without an address.

A life with AIM but no plan to achieve it is like an Envelope with an address but not posted.

If there is turmoil internally, then everything outside seems confused.

The size of your problem is nothing compared to your ability to solve it, but by overestimating the problem you underestimate yourself.

Life Without A F R I E N D Is Like Death Without Witness

A friend in need is a friend indeed. A real friend is one who stays with you forever, through good times and bad. It is said that forgetting a friend is a crime, ignoring him is a shame, liking him is a pleasure and disturbing him is a fundamental right. Friendship is by choice and not like a relative who is by chance and not by choice. In one's life a friend is more reliable than a relative; therefore, it is said that life without a friend is like death without a witness.

One has a limited number of relatives, but he can have a countless number of friends. It depends on how he lives in society, how lively he is, how social he is and how helpful he is. Friendship is always mutual and reciprocal. There is no limit to the love and the sacrifices in a friendship.

There could be good and bad in a friend, what you have to do is to bring out the good in your friends and leave the bad to shrivel up and die.

When To Do What In Life

The creator gave a normal life span of 40 years to humans, animals, birds. Humans thought a life span of 40 years is too little that nothing much could be done in 40 years and hence desired to have more. The animals, on the contrary, thought that a life span of 40 years is too long as it is difficult to fetch food, make shelter, etc. Similarly, the birds also thought that it is too long as they have to migrate from season to season to different places and every day they have to go in search of food, etc. All the creatures went to the Creator and pleaded explaining their difficulties. The creator being very gracious limited the life of animals and birds to 20 years. The humans grabbed the remaining 20 years of the animals and the 20 years sacrificed by the birds. This may be the reason that humans are very healthy and strong for the first 40 years which happen to be their own, as granted by the creator and during the next 20 years usually one talks more and does less just as dogs bark and don't do much work. In the same way, the latter 20 years are spent like owls sitting in one place and watching the world go by. One should therefore lead the first 40 years for the benefit of himself and his family. The next 20 years he should contribute to society in any way he can and the next 20 years he should do charitable work to lead a more meaningful life so that the purpose of his birth is justified.

Never think that anything is impossible for the soul. Never be weak, be strong and you will find infinite strength within yourself. During birth and life, one takes so much from society, and one has to repay not in equal measure with what he has taken but many folds more. Only then will one have satisfaction in the last years of life.

Life Is With Nature, Be Part Of It

To those who see life with loving eyes
   Life is beautiful
   To those who speak with tender care
   Life is peaceful
   To those who help with gentle hands
   Life is full
   And those who care with compassionate hearts
   Life is beyond all measure.

Outside the human world we find perfect peace and tranquility in the rest of the Universe. There is peace in stars, in air, in water, in trees and animals. The whole machinery of creation, excluding the world of man, is running peacefully and does not betray any imbalance or disorder or indiscipline in any respect. Why is human life deprived of this blessing?

Lord made our universe very interesting with Sun, Moon, Sky, Planets, Stars, etc. Water vapor rises from the oceans and turns into clouds; the wind blows these clouds to the distant corners of the earth and, under suitable conditions, the vapor condenses into water and falls on the earth as rain. The rain water in its turn brings dead soil to life and helps the growth of various kinds of food grains and other crops, luxuriant trees and different varieties of fruits and flowers.

Human life is part of nature, and therefore, one has to live with nature and not go against nature. Nature provides Air, Water, Food, Shelter, Clothing and everything that humans need. Human life is similar to other living things but it is more advanced and superior in many respects. Humans can feel, think, talk, work, sleep, and therefore it is precious and has to be utilized for good. Every day is god's gift and should be used as if it is the last day of life; only then will one understand the importance of life. Even though death is certain, no one knows when the end will come and life after death is beyond our imagination. Nothing is certain, and fate follows its destiny. Many a time what looks easy may not be so and what one thinks impossible may become possible. Therefore life becomes more interesting and challenging. One has to be always cautious, attentive, careful and hopeful throughout life.

One could be born in a rich family/royal family or in a poor family but there is no certainty that he will continue in the same status. There could be drastic changes due to many factors. This makes life interesting.

We may never know why the creator gave us life; we can only try to make the best out of our life and leave the rest to destiny.

It is, therefore, essential to lead a meaningful life doing only good things. Life is full of beauty; love your life and use it to the fullest potential.

Some people love to sleep because in that state all the miseries, sorrows and sufferings are absent and they are in a state of bliss. If a person suffers from insomnia, he will not be lively, or happy. In the past, man used to rise when the sun rose and go to sleep when the sun set, but as the years passed he stayed up late at night and then obviously got up late the next morning. Present day youth go to sleep very late at night and get up very late in the morning; this is against nature. People who work at night and sleep late in the morning are going against nature will sooner or later find themselves facing adverse consequences.

The basic needs of life -Air, Water, Shelter, Clothing and Food - are provided by nature; and therefore, one has to be with nature. Life will not be convenient even if one of the five is absent; all are essential in everybody's life. Nature provides all these abundantly.

Everything comes from nature and returns to nature. The world of nature is nothing but the energy of that supreme lord who is the creator.

Unfortunately one thinks that the material body is the real self. The body ages and becomes old, and one day it has to die, but the soul will not die. It will part from the body and reach the hands of the creator.

One has to realize the reality and move from darkness to light. Light refers to knowledge and darkness refers to the state of spiritual ignorance. One has to aim for and achieve inner happiness, only then can permanent happiness be derived.

Do Good Things And You Are Answerable To The Creator

By the grace of the creator, you were born as a human that is a superior being in this universe. Being so precious, we must always strive to be good, think positive, love nature, learn to share and live with others, be creative, work honestly, be honest, be genuine and be affectionate towards fellow beings. Always speak good things, listen to good things and do good things. Have good habits and good friends. There are many educated people in the world today but intelligent ones are very few. We should be like small children who are always happy as they are pure, don't have evil thoughts, and can sleep peacefully.

Every living being in this universe lives by the grace of the creator, and therefore, no one should hate another person, and should learn to live with everybody. There is peace only when you share with others and live with others: think of the welfare of others by forgetting the self.

Man is essentially individualistic. There is nothing wrong with this, but he should remember that others are also like him; then there will be no confusion, no threat, fight, disturbance or war. One has to treat everyone alike regardless of race, religion, color, caste, economic or social status.

Many times there is a smile on the face but there is no inner happiness. We must learn to control our feelings and enjoy the present, look for a better tomorrow. One day your life will flash before your eyes; make sure it is worth watching. We cannot free ourselves of the attendant miseries accompanying this mortal life cycle of birth and death by amassing wealth.

Always be alert against the four sins which the tongue is prone to commit: speaking falsehood, speaking ill of others, back biting, talking too much. Control these tendencies.

In This World, There Are Four Types Of People, Everywhere

1) There are people that make things happen.
2) There are people that watch things happen.
3) There are people that wonder what happened.
4) There are people that don't know anything happened.
   By the by, what category you belong to?

The seven sins of life are

1.   *Politics with out principle*
2.   *Commerce with out morality*
3.   *Wealth with out work*
4.   *Education with out character*
5.   *Science with out humanity*
6.   *Pleasure with out conscience*
7.   *Worship with out sacrifice*

ABCD OF LIFE

'A'lways 'B'e 'C'ool, 'D'ont have 'E'go with 'F'riends, 'G'ive up 'H'urting 'I'ncidences, 'J'ust 'K'eep 'L'oving 'M'ankind, 'N'ever 'O'mit 'P'rayers, 'Q'uitely 'R'emember Lord. "'S'peak 'T'ruth, 'U'se 'V'alid 'W'ords 'X'press 'Y'our 'Z'eal.

TRUE LOVE IS ETERNAL

Cherish the Love when you have got the chance
       For once it leaves you, it would be difficult to get it back.
       Don't let Love be only a memory to you.

Life Is...

- Wealth and power are fruits of life. Family and friends are roots of life. A tree can live without fruits, but not without roots.

- Life sometimes takes unknown turn; don't be afraid to go through it. Someday that turn will take you to untouched heights on top of the world.

- Life is better when you are happy but life is at its best when other people are happy because of you. Be inspired, give love and share your smile with everyone.

- Life is an ECHO. All comes back, the good, the bad, the false, the true, so give the world the best you have and the best will come back to you.

- Life is a novel of mystery. You never know which page will bring a good twist in the story. Keep on reading because happiness comes when it is most unexpected.

- Do not go through life, grow through life. Life never leaves you empty; it always replaces everything you lost. If it asks you to put something down, it is because it wants you to pick up something better.

- No candle loses its light while lighting other candles never stop sharing, caring and helping others because it makes your life even more meaningful.

- Life is a daily cleansing; negativity must be washed away, if you wish to attract positive experiences to your life.

- In life you get a lot to loose and very little to choose. So whenever you get chance to choose, do it wisely and make it sure that you never loose what you choose.

- Diet plan of life- Eat your words, swallow your pride, digest teaching of guru/teacher, eliminate your ego.

- Do not worry if others do not understand you; worry only if you cannot understand yourself? Live in your passion and love your life.

- Past of ice is water; future of ice is water too; so live like ice. No regrets for past, no worries about future.

- Life is like a coin. Pleasure and pain are two sides. Only one side is visible at a time but remember other side is also waiting for its turn.

- Every day is special if you think so. Every moment is memorable if you feel so. Everyone is unique if you see and life is wonderful if you live so.

- Birth was not our choice. Death is also not our choice. But the way we live our life is absolutely our choice. Enjoy it and make each day memorable.

- Anybody can love a rose, but it takes a great deal to love a leaf. Do not love someone just because the person is beautiful, but love the one who can make your life beautiful.
- Life is really nothing without love. Give everyone your love, but do not expect it back because "It is not a deal. It is a feel"
- Every test in life makes us bitter or better. Every problem comes to make us or break us. Choice is ours. Whether to become victim or victor.
- Life is at its weakest when there are more doubts than trust, but life is at its strongest when you learn how to trust even if there are doubts.
- Unexpected results and problems are part of life. Never lose hope in any condition, because darkness of night always finishes with light of the day.
- Patience and silence are powerful energies. Patience makes you mentally strong. Silence makes you emotionally strong. Have a strong and healthy life.
- It is a long journey between human being and being human. Let us travel at least one step daily to cover the distance.
- We cannot tailor-make the situations in life. We can tailor-make the attitude to face those situations.
- Two gems of life: 1. Live life to express and not to impress, 2. Do not strive to make your presence noticed, just make your absence felt.
- Like birds, let us leave behind what we do not need to carry- grudges, sadness, pain, fear and regrets. Life is beautiful, enjoy it. Happy times all the time.

- Do not be so much emotional in your life that it hurts you and do not get too much practical in life that it hurts others.

- Live with no excuses and love with no regrets. When life gives you a hundred reasons to cry, show life that you have thousand reasons to Smile.

- Life is a compromise between your feelings and reality. At every stage you have to quit your feelings and accept the reality.

- One good deed a day works in life like a thread woven each day in the quilt that will keep us warm in winters.

- Life is not a sharp knife to cut all those bad memories. But life is a needle to weave golden thread of sweet memories.

- Mistake is a single page of life but relation is a complete book, so do not lose a full book for single page.

- Audience sees a Joker as a comedian, but the Joker sees himself as a performer. Life is also like a circus. The way you see yourself, may not be the way others see.

Life Is Romantic

If you want to see the power of God, see the SUN,

If you want to know the beauty of God, see the MOON,

If you want to know the best creation of God, see the MIRROR, You see yourself and that is the best creation God, Life is so romantic and see the sun raise or sun set, see the full moon, see the stars, sea the river flow, hear the ocean, feel the air, relish the pure water, feel the heat in cold weather and realize how good the life is and enjoy every second which is precious which never comes back in your life.

If you have a young heart to enjoy the life never cease to amaze you.

Happy Moments Of Your Life

The best moments in your life, just comes and by the time you really think of, it will go away and it becomes a memory. On the contrary, if any thing happens bad, you will remember for long time and it pains you, even if you want to forget, you can not do it easily, cultivate the habit of forgetting the bad things and remembering the good things to enjoy the life which is very precious.

True friends come in the good times
when we tell them to,
and come in the bad times.... without calling."

1) "Never make friends with people who are above or below you in status. Such friendships will never give you any happiness."

2) "Treat your kid like a darling for the first five years. For the next five years, scold them. By the time they turn sixteen, treat them like a friend. Your grown up children are your best friends."

3) "Books are as useful to a stupid person as a mirror is useful to a blind person."

4) "Education is the best friend. An educated person is respected everywhere. Education beats the beauty and the youth."

Life Is A Candle In The Hands Of God

Entire water in the ocean can never sink a ship, Unless it gets inside. All the pressures of life can never hurt you unless you let them in.

A small candle was carried by a man who was climbing the stairs of a lighthouse. On their way up, the candle asked the man, "Where are you going?"

"We are going to the top of this lighthouse and give signals to the big ships on the ocean," the man answered.

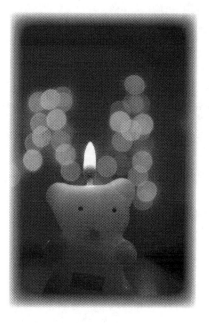

"What? How could it be possible for me with my small light to give signals to those big ships? They will never be able to see my light," replied the candle weakly".

"That's your part. If your light is small, let it be.

All you have to do is keep burning and leave the rest to me," said the man.

A little later, they arrived at the top of the lighthouse where there was a big lamp.

Then the man lit the lamp with the light of the candle and instantly, the place shone so brightly that the ships on the ocean could see its light.

Very often in life we are worried about our limitations and we stay away from allowing God to use us.

God does not look at our abilities or inabilities; He is only looking for our availability.

You should bear in mind that your life is like a small candle in God's most powerful hands.

All your abilities and expertise will remain as small as the small candle unless you make yourself available to God.

On the contrary, even if your light is just a small flick, if you surrender your life to God,

He will make use of it most meaningfully in a mighty and just way that will bring blessings to many people.

Every Thing Happens
For Good In Life

An old farmer had an old horse for tilling his fields. One day the horse escaped into the hills and, when all the farmer's neighbours sympathised with the old man over his bad luck, the farmer replied, 'Bad luck? Good luck? Who knows?'

A week later the horse returned with a herd of wild horses from the hills and this time the neighbors congratulated the farmer on his good luck. His reply was, 'Good luck? Bad luck? Who knows?'

Then, when the farmer's son attempted to tame one of the wild horses, he fell off its back and broke his leg. Everyone thought this was very bad luck. Not the farmer, whose only reaction was, 'Bad luck? Good luck? Who knows?'

Some weeks later the army marched into the village and forced every able-bodied youth they found there by law to serve in the army. When they saw the farmer's son with his broken leg they let him off. Now was that good luck? Bad luck? Who knows? Everything happens for good, what happens bad may be for future good.

What is happiness?

I will share the following story to answer this question: one POOR lady and two boys were sitting on the muddy floor of a hut with a bowl of rice and little salt. Three of them were taking one grasp of rice from one bowl and one fingertip of salt as vegetable and their eyes were twinkling in joy and excitement and for the first time I realized what happiness means!

When I think of happiness I think of them, their rolling eyes while putting the handful of rice in their mouth. When I get scared of what I might lose in the process – job, money, stuffs, clothes, costly gifts, even near and dear ones, I think of them as my reference point.

If they, without anything, can be happy, why not us?! It's not the outside goodies that can make you and me happy, it's the choice we make on everyday basis about being happy or not being happy. Lots of reasons we can find out if we just try to back our choice, either happiness or unhappiness. But it never depends on others or a circumstance or a tragedy. It's a way of living and a way of life! And the empowering thing is – We can choose it!

VALUE OF SILENCE _ My missing watch:

I had lost my watch once, which is valuable and had sentimental value. After searching high and low among the hay for a long while, I gave up and took the help of a group of children playing outside the field. I promised them that the person who found it would be rewarded.

Hearing this, the children hurried inside the barn, went through and around the entire stack of hay but still could not find the watch. A little boy came to me and asked to be given another chance.

After a while the little boy came out with the watch in his hand! I was surprised and asked the boy how he succeeded where the rest had failed.

The boy replied, "I did nothing but sit on the ground and listen. In the silence, I heard the ticking of the watch and just looked for it in that direction."

Moral: A peaceful mind can think well than a worked up mind.

Allow a few minutes of silence to your mind every day, and see, how sharply It helps you to set your life the way you expect it to be...!

ARE YOU GOD?

Last week on a cold day a little boy, about 10-years-old, was standing before a shoe store on the roadway, barefooted, peering through the window, and shivering with cold.

My daughter approached the young boy and said, 'Hello, why are you in such deep thought staring in that window?'

'I was asking God to give me a pair of shoes, was the boy's reply, and it is his dream that he should wear that shoes.

My daughter took him by the hand, went into the store, and asked the salesman to give him the one he liked. She also gave a shall and She patted him on the head and said, your dream has come true and be happy.

As she turned to go, the astonished kid caught her by the hand and looking up into her face, with tears in his eyes, asked her:

'Are you God's wife?'

She said, 'No'

Then he said, 'You must be God's relative'.

LOGICAL THINKING

MORAL OF THE STORY: Most complex problems do have a solution.. It is only that we don't attempt to think. A man is but a product of his thoughts... M. K. Gandhi.

A farmer took money from moneylender. He could not repay back, money lender had an eye on farmer's daughter. So he proposed a bargain.

Both the farmer and his daughter were horrified by the proposal. The cunning moneylender suggested that they let Providence decide the matter. He told them that he would put a black pebble and a white pebble into an empty moneybag. Then the daughter would have to pick one pebble from the bag. If she picked the black pebble, she would become his wife and her father's debt would be forgiven. If she picked the white pebble she need not marry him and debt would still be forgiven. But if she refused to pick a pebble, her father would be thrown into jail.

The moneylender bent over to pick up two pebbles. As he picked them up, the sharp-eyed daughter noticed that he had picked up two black pebbles and put them into the bag. He then asked the girl to pick a pebble from the bag. See how the un educated village girl had a logical thinking –

The girl put her hand into the bag and drew out a pebble. Without looking at it, she fumbled and let it fall onto the pebble-strewn path where it immediately became lost among all the other pebbles. 'Oh, how clumsy of me,' she said. 'But never mind, if you look into the bag for the one that is left, you will be able to tell which pebble I picked.' Since the remaining pebble is black, it must be assumed that she had picked the white one. And since the moneylender dared not admit his dishonesty, the girl changed what seemed an impossible situation into an extremely advantageous one.

THE ATTITUDE

Why do we have so many temples, if God is everywhere?
Ans: Air is everywhere but we still need a fan to feel it.

When you Trust somebody, completely trust him, at the end you will learn a lesson for life or you will have a good friend.

Life is not about the people who act true to your face, it is all about the people who remain true behind your back.

Army person said, we are surrounded by enemies, Major said excellent, we can attach in any direction.

Every moment, every situation, every issue and every concern has a positive side, find it and bring it to your life.

IT'S SO TOUCHING:

Conversation between Pencil and Eraser:

Pencil: I'm sorry… Eraser: For what? You didn't do anything wrong.

Pencil: Whenever I made a mistake, you're always there to erase it. But as you make my mistake vanish, you lose a part of yourself. You get smaller and smaller each time.

Eraser: That's true. But I don't really mind. You see, I was made to do this.

Parents are like the eraser and children are like pencil, whenever their children do mistakes, they have to correct them, train them, sometimes along the way...they get hurt, and become older and eventually pass on. Though their children will eventually find someone new (Spouse), but parents are still happy with what they do for their children.

Don't Have Email ID If You Want To Become Millionaire

A jobless man applied for the position of "office boy" at a big mall.

The HR manager interviewed him then watched him cleaning the floor as a test.

"You are employed." He said." Give me your e-mail address and I'll send you the application to fill in, as well as date when you may start."

The man replied "But I don't have a computer, neither an email."

I'm sorry", said the HR manager, "If you don't have an email, that means you do not exist. And who doesn't exist, cannot have the job."

The man left with no hope at all. He didn't know what to do, with only $10 in his pocket. He then decided to go to the supermarket and buy a 10Kg tomato crate. He then sold the tomatoes in a door to door round. In less than two hours, he succeeded to double his capital.

He repeated the Operation three times, and returned home with $60.

The man realized that he can survive this Way, and started to go everyday earlier, and return late Thus, his money doubled or tripled every day. Soon, he bought a cart, then a truck, then he had his own fleet of delivery vehicles.

5 years later, the man is one of the biggest food retailers in the US .

He started to plan his family's future, and decided to have a life insurance.

He called an insurance broker, and chose a protection plan. When the conversation was concluded, the broker asked him his email. The man replied, "I don't have an email". The broker answered curiously, "You don't have an email, and yet have succeeded to build an empire. Can you imagine what you could have been if you had an email?!!"

The man thought for a while and replied, "Yes, I'd be an office boy at a big mall!"

Moral of the story:

M1 - Internet is not the solution to your life.

M2 - If you don't have Internet, and work hard, you can be a millionaire.

M3 - If you received this message by email, you are closer to being an office boy, than a millionaire.

Spirit Of Handicap

It was a sports stadium. Eight Children were standing on the track to participate in the running event.

* Ready! * Steady! * Bang!!!

With the sound of Toy pistol, all eight girls started running. Hardly had they covered ten to fifteen steps, one of the smaller girls slipped and fell down. Due to bruises and pain she started crying. When other seven girls heard this sound, they stopped running, stood for a while and turned back. They all ran back to the place where the girl fell down. One among them bent, picked and kissed the girl gently and enquired 'Now pain must have reduced'. All seven girls lifted the girl who fell down, pacified her, two of them held the girl firmly and they all eight joined hands together and walked together and reached the winning post. Officials were shocked. Clapping of thousands of spectators filled the stadium. Many eyes were filled with tears and perhaps it had reached the GOD even! YES. This happened in Hyderabad [INDIA], recently! The sport was conducted by National Institute of Mental Health [NIMH]. All these special girls had come to participate in this event and they are spastic children. Yes, they were mentally retarded.

Sleeping Is Very Essential In Life

Sleeping late and waking up too late will disrupt the process of removing unnecessary chemicals. Aside from that, midnight to 4:00 am is the time when the bone marrow produces blood. Therefore, have a good sleep and don't sleep late.

Health - IMPORTANCE OF SLEEPING:

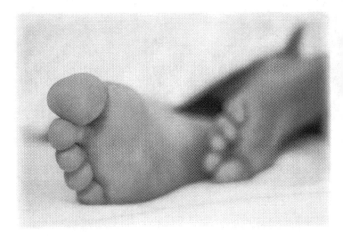

Reasons for sleeping and waking up early.

- **Evening at 9 - 11pm:** is the time for eliminating unnecessary/ toxic chemicals (detoxification) from the antibody system (lymph nodes). This time duration should be spent by relaxing or listening to music. If during this time a housewife is still in an unrelaxed state such as washing the dishes or monitoring children doing their homework, this will have a negative impact on health.

- **Evening at 11pm - 1am:** is the detoxification process in the liver, and ideally should be done in a deep sleep state.

- **Early morning 1 - 3am:** detoxification process in the gall, also ideally done in a deep sleep state.

- **Early morning 3 - 5am:** detoxification in the lungs. Therefore there will sometimes be a severe cough for cough sufferers during this time. Since the detoxification process had reached the respiratory tract, there is no need to take cough medicine so as not to interfere with toxin removal process.

- **Morning 5 - 7am:** detoxification in the colon, you should empty your bowel.

- **Morning 7 - 9am:** absorption of nutrients in the small intestine, you should be having breakfast at this time. Breakfast should be earlier, before 6:30am, for those who are sick. Breakfast before 7:30am is very beneficial to those wanting to stay fit. Those who always skip breakfast, they should change their habits, and it is still better to eat breakfast late until 9 - 10am rather than no meal at all.

Who Is Rich & Who Are Poor

A Rich father takes his son to remote village to make him understand, what it means being POOR:

Son and father spend three days and three nights in the village. Back in the car, father asks his son, what his experience is – Son says GOOD.

Father asks his son whether he has learnt anything in these three days:

Son replied :

We have only one dog and they have several. We have one treated pool, they have a river of clean water and several kinds of fish. We have electric light in our garden and they have stars and moon in their garden. We have wall at the end of our garden; their garden is till your eyes can view.

We listen to music in CD's and they are entertained by birds and creatures.

We have microwave to heat up and they use wood and the food is tasty.

We use Alarms and Gates but they use friends and birds instead of alarms.

We are connected to laptops, TV's internet, cell phones; they are connected to Horizon, skies, greenery, animals and family.

Father was impressed with his son's understanding of things and Son summarises that what I saw is full of richness and we are very poor of all these things.

Life Is A Gift

There was a blind girl who hated herself just because she was blind.

She hated everyone, except her loving boyfriend. He was always there for her. She said that if she could only see the world, she would marry her boyfriend.

One day, someone donated a pair of eyes to her and then she could see everything, including her boyfriend. Her boyfriend asked her, "now that you can see the world, will you marry me?"

The girl was shocked when she saw that her boyfriend was blind too, and refused to marry him. Her boyfriend walked away in tears, and later wrote a letter to her saying:

"Just take care of my eyes dear."

This is how human brain changes when the status changes.

Only few remember what life was before, and who's always been there even in the most painful situations

Life Is A Gift, Today before you think of saying an unkind word– think of someone who can't speak. Before you complain about the taste of your food– think of someone who has nothing to eat.

Before you complain about your husband or wife– think of someone who is crying out to God for a companion.

Today before you complain about life– think of someone who went too early to heaven. Before you complain about your children– think of someone who desires children but they're child lesss.

Before you argue about your dirty house, someone didn't clean or sweep– think of the people who are living in the streets.

Before whining about the distance you drive– think of someone who walks the same distance with his feet.

And when you are tired and complain about your job– think of the unemployed, the disabled and those who wished they had your job. But before you think of pointing the finger or condemning another– remember that not one of us is without sin and we all answer to one maker.

And when depressing thoughts seem to get you down– put a smile on your face and thank God you're alive and still around.

Life Is A Gift – Live It, Enjoy It, Celebrate It, And Fulfill It...

Life is a compromise between your feelings and reality. At every stage you have to quit your feelings and accept the reality.

You are born without anything but you die with your name. So that name must not be a word only, it must be a history.

Do not cheat the one who believes you- Quran. Do not forget the one who helped you - Geetha. Do not hate the one who loved you – Bible.

Never reply when you are angry, never make a promise when you are happy and never make a decision when you are sad.

When you know Truth stands with you, it doesn't matter who stands against you.

Life is not about finding the right person but creating the right relationship. It's not how we care in the beginning but how much we care till ending.

Everyone asks for a miracle, some a house, some a car and some for love. Be happy with what you have and remember: 'Your miracle is that you are alive today'.

When flood comes "fish eat ants". When flood goes, "ants eat fish". Time matters. God gives opportunity to everyone.

Mind & Umbrella are useful only when they are open, otherwise. They increase your burden un-necessarily...

Performance always comes from passion and not from pressure so be passionate. Love what you do and do what you love.

The best thing in life is having people who know all your mistakes & weaknesses. And still think "You are special".!

Divine blessings come as a surprise but, how much we receive depends on how much our heart believes! Be blessed beyond your expectation.

"The Single finger that wipes your tears during your bad times is much better than the ten fingers that come together to clap on your success."

***

Person who has anger doesn't require enemy, person who has knowledge doesn't require wealth, person who has kindness doesn't require protection.

***

'Prayers' and 'Seeds' are similar in nature. Both have nothing within, but have the potential of creating everything.

Develop an attitude of gratitude, and give thanks for everything that happens to you, knowing that every step forward is a step toward achieving something bigger and better than your current situation.

***

Every success makes you grow strong, because it teaches you what to do. But every failure makes you stronger, because it also teaches you what not to do.

If people talk behind your back, what does that mean simple. It means you are two steps ahead of them. Think positive and be positive.

***

One of the very true and greatest illusions of life is that.

"We always believe there is more time in tomorrow than today.

Smile And Smile. Miles To Go:20 Benefits Of Smiling

Here are the many social, physical and mental benefits that something as simple as a smile can do!
A smile can...

1. Start your day pleasantly.
2. Make others understand you are in a good mood.
3. Promote positivity in a work environment.
4. Relax your face muscles.
5. Make others put a smile on their face.
6. Tell people that they are going to be okay.
7. Makes you look a lot prettier or more handsome.
8. Reduce all of that stress you might accumulate.
9. Help to boost your immune system.
10. Lower's your blood pressure.
11. Give you a child like innocence.
12. Release serotonin, natural pain killers and endorphins thus making you happy.
13. Make you look younger.
14. Fill you up with positivity and power.
15. Show your understanding side.
16. Say that you can be polite in the hardest of times.
17. Help you live longer.
18. Make you appreciate the little things in life.
19. Make you look at the brighter side of a bad situation.

20. Be contagious to all those around you.

A smile has more wonderful benefits that you could ever think about.

I know that after you've read this, you are smiling now so don't let anything stop it because a smile is like eating 2000 bars of chocolate! So happy smiling!

Points On How To Improve Your Life

Life is not an ipod to listen to your favourite songs. It is a radio, you must adjust yourself to every frequency and enjoy whatever comes in it

Personality:

1. Don't compare your life to others. You have no idea what their journey is all about.
2. Don't have negative thoughts of things you cannot control. Instead invest your energy in the positive present moment
3. Don't over do; keep your limits
4. Don't take yourself seriously; no one else does
5. Don't waste your precious energy on gossip
6. Dream more while you are awake
7. Envy is a waste of time. You already have all you need..
8. Forget issues of the past. Don't remind your partner of his/her mistakes of the past. That will ruin your present happiness.
9. Life is too short to waste time hating anyone. Don't hate others.
10. Make peace with your past so it won't spoil the present

11. No one is in charge of your happiness except you

12. Realize that life is a school and you are here to learn. Problems are simply part of the curriculum that appear and fade away like algebra class but the lessons you learn will last a lifetime.

13. Smile and laugh more

14. You don't have to win every argument. Agree to disagree.

Community:

15. Call your family members often

16. Each day give something good to others

17. Forgive everyone for everything

18. Spend time with people over the age of 70 & under the age of 6

19. Try to make at least three people smile each day

20. What other people think of you is none of your business

21. Your job will not take care of you when you are sick. Your family and friends will. Stay in touch.

Life:

22. Put GOD first in anything and everything that you think, say and do.
23. GOD heals everything
24. Do the right things
25. However good or bad a situation is, it will change
26. No matter how you feel, get up, dress up and show up
27. The best is yet to come
28. Get rid of anything that isn't useful, beautiful or joyful
29. When you wake up alive in the morning, thank GOD for it
30. If you know GOD you will always be happy. So, be happy.

While you practice all of the above, share this knowledge with the people you love, people you school with, people you play with, people you work with and people you live with. Not only will it enrich YOUR life, but also that of those around you.

Remember,

GOOD THINGS ARE FOR US TO SHARE.....!!!!!!

Some Thing More About Life

Life is a time gap between "Date of Birth to Date of Death", is that true? No, Not at all, even animals will live until they die the question is how many TIMES we take birth & death does not matter. The billion dollar question is in what TIME we move out of this LIFE cycle ? do not expect me to explain the sacred text in Bhagavad Gita because you may be a theist or atheist !!!. Believe me there is a LIFE after death, Trust me I can prove it instantly, no mantra, no tantra, no indrajaal (Magic). Let us question ourselves do you know Mahathma Gandhi? Mother Thersa? Edison? Alexander Graham Bell? Wright brothers? Be ready I can arrange you an appointment with them, but you need to pay "Pay peace to meet Gandhij", "Do service to speak to Mother Thersa", "Switch on the electrical bulb to see Edison", "say Hello!! to Alexander Graham Bell", "Book a flight ticket to meet Wright Brothers". And YES there is a big list of great souls who are still living after their death also you can meet them in our daily LIFE.

If you want to LIVE after death? LIVE the LIFE now every second, every moment, every day and in every deed and need. Remember the LIFE candle is burning very fast. To be very practical justify your time in balancing it. What are the classifications of LIFE and how to balance it?

Common question uncommon answer. My research says there are five types of LIFE :

1. Individual LIFE
2. Family LIFE
3. Social LIFE
4. Career LIFE
5. Spiritual LIFE

Let me explain the profound definitions and technique to balance it.

1. Individual LIFE

In this type of LIFE you always think best about yourself, you will maintain self ESTEEM, you will have your own choice of selection, you work only on your will, maintain self-image when mixed with family, social or career. You will have your own tastes, lifestyle, and passion of living. You will have your own thought process and may not be ready to listen to anyone. You will always prove right.

- If anyone of you belongs to this type of LIFE you may not be successful. An individual should have something to share, express love, gratitude, get appreciated, get connected, you cannot share your victory or sadness if you do not have any Family, so Individual LIFE without FAMILY LIFE is not successful.

2. Family LIFE

80% of the world do not know their parents or do not maintain the parental relationship. You should always enjoy the Family role, as a Husband or Wife, Son or daughter, you should vent out the love to the kids in your family fulfill the role of a father, uncle. Remember to justify all the roles in family. If the Family LIFE is happy and complete you will never be disturbed in your career or individual LIFE. get the blessings of entire family.

- If anyone of you belong to this type of LIFE and does not balance your social LIFE then your family LIFE is incomplete, to identify that your family is best in the world you need a social life, so family LIFE without SOCIAL LIFE is not successful.

3. Social LIFE

Indicates your responsibility towards the country welfare, family relationship, may be friends, classmates, bar mates, sports mates, politics etc., should work for the fame, name & game. If you are good individual & have complete family but no justification in social then you are not successful.

- If anyone of you belong to this type of LIFE and does not balance your career LIFE then your social LIFE is incomplete, to prove in social LIFE you also consider your career or business life, so social LIFE without career LIFE is not successful.

4. Career LIFE

As soon as the sun rises we start our race to earn money, fame, name, game plan for the business, money etc., If you need to spend more and fulfill your material desire you have to earn more, nothing wrong but your 100% should not be earning only.

- If you focus 100% on Career LIFE earn more and spend more but do not know the reason why you are earning the money ? you should know the purpose of living, so career LIFE without SPIRITUAL LIFE is not successful.

5. Spiritual LIFE

Nothing is disposable in this earth, every material, every tree, every stone has a reason behind it. Even you have a reason behind living, you should discover the reason and fulfill the requirement, so start questioning yourself see the best in you and THIS IS CALLED AS LIVING AFTER DEATH.

You should balance and justify Individual, Family, Social, Career, Spiritual LIFE in your LIFE.

Undiscovered Yourself

Do you know who you are? Your body is a bag of bones, blood, urine and many other unclean substances. Your SOUL is brighter and powerful than thousands of SUN.

ASTAVAKRA RISHI was very ugly, when he walked his movements were quite peculiar and awkhard. The people normally laughed at him. Janaka Maharaja invited him along with other saintly persons to attend the assembly. As Astavakra entered the assembly, everyone present there started laughing and seeing them the Rishi also started laughing even more loudly.

Janaka Maharaj asked Rishi why he laughing so loudly? Rishi replied that the people around are innocent and are looking his physical status and laughing, they give importance for outward appearance and do not bother for the inner self and the soul. It is simply illusion to place importance on the external temporary body while being oblivious to the external soul dwelling within.

Maharaj realized and made him to sit on his throne and bowed down to him and also accepted him as his spiritual master.

What Is Inside That Counts

"Soft nature of a person does not mean weakness:
Remember : Nothing is softer than water,
but its force can break the strongest of rocks."

There was a man who made a living selling balloons at a fair. He had all colors of balloons, including red, yellow blue, and green.

Whenever business was slow, he would release a helium-filled balloon into the air and when the children saw it go up, they all wanted to buy one. They would come up to him, buy a balloon, and his sales would go up again. He continued this process all day.

One day, he felt someone tugging at his jacket. He turned around and saw a little boy who asked, "If you release a black balloon, would that also fly?" Moved by the boy's concern, the man replied with empathy, "Son, it is not the color of the balloon, it is what is inside that makes it go up."

The same thing applies to our lives. It is what is inside that counts. The thing inside us that makes us go up is our attitude.

Have you ever wondered why some individuals, organizations, or countries are more successful than others?

It is not a secret. These people simply think and act more effectively. They have learned how to do so by investing in the most valuable asset people.

The success of an individual, organization or country, depends on the quality of the person as their people.

Medical & Moral Science

Medical science says, an injury on a tongue heals the quickest.

Moral Science says, an injury caused by a tongue takes the longest time to heal.

ATHMA & PARAMATHMA:

Take one candle ignite it. using the same candle light 100 more. the First candle never looses its Brightness !!!

Energy when given or transferred to other the energy in you will never get drained. All the candles are athma and the first candle is param-athma. so the light in atma and param-athma is same and from same source.

Energy can be drawn through Power of Silence (Meditation). you know lord Shiva is also seen in meditation poster !!! even he needs energy and he will draw frequently by "meditation". all this energy comes from one source (light) in the universe and it is Bindhu (a dot of bright light).

Rivers don't drink water, they carry.
Trees don't eat fruits, they bear.
The Clouds don't bath, they shower.
So be involved in your KARMA
knowing whatever you carry nothing is yours.
Love + Care = Mom & Love + Fear = Dad
Love + Help = Sister & Love + Fight = Brother
Love + Life = Wife / Husband
Love + Care + Fear + Help + Fight + Life = Friend

The Best Cosmetics In Life

TRUTH- for lips
PITY- for eyes
CHARITY- for hands.
SMILE- for face.
LOVE- for heart..
Use them well and make life beautiful......!

SEVEN TIPS FOR MOTIVATION:

1. Set a major goal, but follow a path. The path has mini goals that go in many directions.When you learn to succeed at mini goals, you will be motivated to challenge grand goals.

2. Finish what you start. A half-finished project is of no use to anyone. Quitting is a habit. Develop the habit of finishing self-motivated projects.

3. Socialize with others of similar interest. Mutual support is motivating. We will develop the attitudes of our five best friends. If they are losers, we will be a loser. If they are winners, we will be a winner. To be a cowboy we must associate with cowboys.

4. Learn how to learn. Dependency on others for knowledge supports the habit of procrastination. Man has the ability to learn without instructors. In fact, when we learn the art of self-education we will find, if not create, opportunity to find success beyond our wildest dreams.

5. Harmonize natural talent with interest that motivates. Natural talent creates motivation, motivation creates persistence and persistence gets the job done.

6. Increase knowledge of subjects that inspires. The more we know about a subject, the more we want to learn about it. A self-propelled upward spiral develops.

7. Take risk. Failure and bouncing back are elements of motivation. Failure is a learning tool. No one has ever succeeded at anything worthwhile without a string of failures.

There Are Two Types Of People In This World

The first is internally-motivated; they set goals for themselves and push themselves towards their goals on their own. This group of people is usually those who do not believe in religions.

The second group is one that is externally-motivated; they rely on external motivation - religion, the promise of reward etc. This group of people is usually those who firmly believe in religion.

Working with the different groups requires a slightly different approach to the task. When working with the latter group, all you have to do is reward him or her with something. Praise him or her. When working with the former group, put him in comparison with another person who is weaker than him or her. He or she would do the rest.

There are many cases of talents & potential being wasted, just because they did not develop it further. I heard of this student whose mother allowed him to go out with his friends only once a year. Naturally he has close-to-zero social lifestyle, and any talents he might have would be lost. Perhaps he is good at drawing? Playing piano?

So depending on which group you belong to, you can do different things to self-motivate. For the former group, start comparing yourself with weaker peers (but don't get too big-headed). For the latter group, start writing down the praises that others gave you. Remember, your brain is a powerful thing. You definitely have a talent. If you've discovered it, don't waste it. Motivate yourself to develop it further. For those of you who haven't discovered it, don't be discouraged. You will find it one day.

Thanks Giving

I dreamt that I went to Heaven and an angel was showing me around. We walked side-by-side inside a large workroom filled with angels. My angel guide stopped in front of the first section and said, "This is the Receiving Section. Here, all petitions to God said in prayer are received."

I looked around in this area, and it was terribly busy with so many angels sorting out petitions written on voluminous paper sheets and scraps from people all over the world. Then we moved on down a long corridor until we reached the second section.

The angel then said to me, "This is the Packaging and Delivery Section. Here, the graces and blessings the people asked for are processed and delivered to the living persons who asked for them." I noticed again how busy it was there. There were many angels working hard at that station, since so many blessings had been requested and were being packaged for delivery to Earth.

Finally at the farthest end of the long corridor we stopped at the door of a very small station. To my great surprise, only one angel was seated there, idly doing nothing. "This is the Acknowledgment Section," my angel friend quietly admitted to me. He seemed embarrassed.

"How is it that there is no work going on here?" I asked.

"So sad," the angel sighed. "After people receive the blessings that they asked for, very few send back acknowledgments."

"How does one acknowledge God's blessings?" I asked.

"Simple," the angel answered. Just say, "Thank you, Lord."

"What blessings should they acknowledge?" I asked.

"If you have food in the refrigerator, clothes on your back, a roof overhead and a place to sleep you are richer than 75% of this world. If you have money in the bank, in your wallet, and spare change in a dish, you are among the top 8% of the world's wealthy, and if you get this on your own computer, you are part of the 1% in the world who has that opportunity."

"If you woke up this morning with more health than illness.. You are more blessed than the many who will not even survive this day."

"If you have never experienced the fear in battle, the loneliness of imprisonment, the agony of torture, or the pangs of starvation... You are ahead of 700 million people in the world."

"If you can attend a church without the fear of harassment, arrest, torture or death you are envied by, and more blessed than, three billion people in the world."

"If your parents are still alive and still married.... you are very rare." "If you can hold your head up and smile, you are not the norm, you're unique to all those in doubt and despair......."

"Ok," I said. "What now? How can I start?"

The Angel said, "If you can read this message, you just received a double blessing in that someone was thinking of you as very special and you are more blessed than over two billion people in the world who cannot read at all."

Have a good day, count your blessings, and if you care to, pass this along to remind everyone else how blessed we all are.........

What Has Happened In My Life

The following real instances which happened have wonderful shades of emotions. These will remove some wrong misconceptions that we have about the people and life in general.

1. One's, when I slipped on the wet tile floor a boy in a wheelchair caught me before I slammed my head on the ground. He said, "Believe it or not, that's almost exactly how I injured my back 3 years ago.

2. When I was upset on my failure, my father told me, "Just go for it and give it a try! You don't have to be a professional to build a successful product. Amateurs started Google and Apple. Professionals built the Titanic.

3. I asked my mentor – a very successful business man in his 70's – what are his top 3 tips for success? He smiled and said, "Read something no one else is reading, think something no one else is thinking, and do something no one else is doing.

4. I interviewed my grandmother for part of a research paper I'm Working on for my Psychology class. When I asked her to define success in her own words, she said, "Success is when you look back at your life and the memories make you smile".

5. Other day, I watched my dog get run over by a car, I sat on the side of the road holding him and crying. And just before he died, he licked the tears off my face.

6. When we all assembled at my mother's hospital bed, my mother uttered her last coherent words before she died. She simply said, "I feel so loved right now. We should have got together like this more often."

7. My friend kissed his dad on the forehead as he passed away in a small hospital bed. About 5 seconds after he passed, he realized that it was the first time that he had given him a kiss.

8. I witnessed a 27-year-old breast cancer patient laughing hysterically at her 2-year-old daughter's antics, I suddenly realized that I need to stop complaining about my life and start celebrating it again.

"In Life Failure is not the Real End, But It Can be the Real Beginning of Success"

Human Life is Ultimate:

As soon you get up, thank god for giving such a precious life, take a vow that you will not get wasted, you are going to use all energy to develop yourself, to achieve enlightenment for the benefit of human beings, always think good for others. Life is precious as you make it; Life is invaluable, human life is supreme. In harmony, all plants and animals support the cycle of living by providing food, clean air, pure water and what not. The knowledge and wisdom we grasp, acquire intelligence, our understanding, our observation makes human life supreme.

You will know how precious life is when you are experiencing near death, you will remember what the things you did and didn't do are. That's the time when you will know how your life is important. We have only one soul and we will grow old as time flies we will not be able to change our age. We can't do things we did when we're old.

The preciousness of life can only be judged from an inward point of view.

Life is precious as long as you make something of it, whatever that may be. The preservation of life is thus means to an end. To love, to hate, to touch, to rate against others in a grand rat race. For better or worse. Even just to find a goal in life makes a life. "The value of a <u>human life</u> is beyond any reckoning".

Karma & Reincarnation: Karma literally means 'deed' or 'act'. The veda's tell us if we sow goodness, we will reap goodness and if we sow evil, we reap evil. One is evil, which is anger, envy, jealousy, sorrow, regret, greed, arrogance, self-pity, guilt, resentment, inferiority, lies, false, superiority, and ego which are indeed very bad and on the contrary the other is good, which is joy, peace, love, hope, serenity, humility, kindness, benevolence, empathy, generosity, truth, compassion and faith. Karma refers to the totality of our actions in this birth and previous birth and that alone determines the future.

Necessary that karma rebounds immediately. Some accumulate and return unexpectedly in this or other births. Reincarnation – After death the soul departs and goes the next and continues birth after birth till and until get Moksha. It is seen in many miracles, that there is connection with the last birth or even with the births prior to that. The bondage of the obligations of the past births will lead to present life. One has to realize and do only good deeds. On death we leave behind physical body and continue evolving in the inner world until we enter into other birth. We are therefore not the body we live but the immortal soul. After death, we continue to exist in unseen worlds, enjoying or suffering the harvest of earthly deeds. Reincarnation ceases where karma is resolved and moksha is attained.

WHAT HAPPENS AFTER DEATH?

One has to ponder how the human infant forms and develops in the tiny workshop of the mother's womb. The father has no hand in this wonderful process nor has the mother anything to do. Two live cells which cannot be seen with bare eyes meet and form a pouch, they draw blood which supplies iron, sulpher, phosphorus and other essential substances in requisite proportions. It will form into a lump of flesh, and then develops various organs and parts of the body, the eyes, ears, brain, and heart in the appropriate places. The bones and muscles grow in proportion, the embryo then acquires life and develops the senses and God puts *atma* into the body and it enters mother earth as a human being. At death the *atma* departs and the body remains. After death, the body is buried in the ground and every particle of it mingles with the dust, or it is burned and the ashes vanish in the air, or are devoured by fishes or dissolve in the sea water: whichever the case, you will not be able to escape the arm of the divine Law. For the air, the soil, the water and the fish are all subject to the command of God.

HAPPYNESS IS HIDDEN WITH YOU JUST REMOVE YOUR WORRIES:

If you see the moon ..... You see the beauty of God ..... If you see the Sun ..... You see the power of God ..... And .... If you see the Mirror ..... You see the best Creation of GOD .... So Believe in YOURSELF..... :) :) :).

"Our life is like an echo. We get back what we give. When we do good to others, you are best to yourself. Whether it is our thoughts, actions or behavior, sooner or later they return and with great accuracy."

WHERE IS HAPPINESS?

Charlie Chaplin's Heart touching words-Nothing is permanent in this world, not even our Troubles...The most wasted day in life is the day we have not laughed

It has been observed that permanent and absolute happiness cannot be procured from any of the objects in the world. The source of happiness is inside oneself. There are only two sides: inside and outside. If it is not to be found outside, then it has to be inside, and one has to learn the way to go inside and find it.

You have to withdraw all your senses from the objects of this world and cease thinking about one's health, body, wife, children, money, friends, and enemies. Once the outside is closed, only then you can enter inside. Once this is achieved, you will be full of peace, happiness and brightness. Once self realization is achieved, there will be no sorrows and sufferings, only permanent bliss.

In life there are two permanent things: the body and the *atman* or soul. If *athman*/soul get into the body, there is life, and if *athman* gets away from the body, there is no life – only a dead body. Our souls are more brilliant and powerful than the sun. The body is nothing but a bag of bones, blood, urine, and other unclean substances. The mind is also part of body but it is different from the soul. What you aspire for and get is only momentary pleasure: not permanent.

There is only one Supreme God, the same god for Hindus, Christians, Muslims and others. One should understand this and treat everyone alike, never to harm or criticize. Everyone has a soul and that is of the creator; the soul is nothing but god. Therefore, god is within oneself.

There is no other way to become happy in this or any other world. Rebirth is certain, and everything in the next birth depends upon what one has done in one's previous birth. That is the reason why whether one is born in a beggar family or a royal family, his future depends on his *karma*.

Swami Vivekananda said, "What we want is strength, so believe in yourself, make your nerves strong; what we want is muscles of iron and nerves of steel. We have wept long enough; enough is enough, no more weeping, stand on your feet."

Men should be practical, physically strong. A dozen such lions will conquer the world, not millions of sheep.

Don't hate anybody, the hatred which comes from you will someday come back to you?

Love others and love will come back to you.

First keep peace with yourself, then you can also bring peace to others.

There are no short cuts to achieve success.

Both rain and sunshine are needed to make a rainbow. Both joy and sorrow are needed to make life truly beautiful and colorful.

FACTS OF LIFE

Have you ever asked yourself the question "How did it get so late so soon?", while you got caught up in everyday hustle and bustle you completely forgot to live? Take time to realize what you want and need. Take time to take risks. Take time to love, laugh, cry, learn, and forgive. Life is shorter than it often seems.

***

To be an average performer, we need good network and friends, but to be very successful performer we need the competition and enemies.

***

Lucky is the one, who gets the opportunity,
Brilliant is the one who creates the opportunity,
Winner is the one who uses the opportunity.

***

Our Life begins with our CRY
Our Life ends with others CRY
Try to utilize this gap in laugh as much as possible
Wish to see the smile on your face always, every time.

***

LIFE is Valuable, Vibrant, Victorious, Vivacious, Versatile, Virtuous, Visionary, Valiant, Refined, Responsible, Resonant, Rejoicing, Resplendent, Renowned, Resolute, Rewarding, Reverent, Remarkable, Recommendable.

***

PROBLEMS ARE THERE EVERY WHERE

No one is free from problems. The volume and value of problems depending upon the individual personality and his/her surrounding environment. Every problems has its own solutions, and also necessity is the mother of invention. it is worth to mentioned here that if the problems couldn't solved by us, the nature will take care, the depth and intensity is differ from period to period. If no problems to us, or if we come across no problems in our life we become incomplete/inefficient/lazy man. To become complete/effective/efficient/vibrant man one should see all the dimensions in his/her life. One should not escape from the problems, face it and overcome that gives lot of practical real experience. Let us contribute and take risk for the good of society and well being of the environment. When we think perfect and clear, the God gives us super-natural-will-power-path to carryout required event.

BE SUCESSFUL

The reason of people being successful is: "They walk the extra mile beyond the point from where the unsuccessful people return."

"Worry is a total waste of time. It does not change anything but surely keeps us very busy doing nothing."

***

BE GOOD HUMAN BEING

Calmness under stress and Courtesy under provocation are not the signs of weakness but rarest of human qualities. "Be a good human being".

We are disappointed because we are standing under orange tree expecting mango. "Either we should change our expectation or change the tree."

***

STAY COOL

"It is true that every effort is not converted into success but it is equally true that success does not come without efforts."

Iron is very strong metal but it becomes weak when it is hot. So always stay cool and happy in any situation. You will always be strong in life."

***

HEART

"Heart is the only machine that works without any repair for years" Always keep it happy, whether it is yours or "others".

"Never raise your voice, just improve the quality of your arguments". Kind words can be short and easy to speak but their echoes are truly endless."

***

A man prayed to God: "I Want Happiness" God said: First remove " I " that 's ego, then remove "Want" that's desire, and see you are left with only "Happiness".

***

FOLLOW THESE FOR BETTER LIFE

Answer the phone by LEFT ear.
Do not drink coffee TWICE a day.
Do not take pills with COOL water.
Do not have HUGE meals after 5pm.
Reduce the amount of OILY food you consume.
Drink more WATER in the morning, less at night.
Keep distance from your hand phone CHARGERS.
Do not use headphones/earphone for LONG period of time.
Best sleeping time is from 10pm at night to 6am in the morning.
Do not lie down immediately after taking medicine before sleeping.
When battery is down to the LAST grid/bar, do not answer the phone as the radiation is 1000 times.

***

SUCESSFUL EXIT

Always have a successful exit than a favorable entrance because what matters is not being clapped when we arrive but being remembered when we leave.

Change in life is a natural process but to adjust and fine tune ourselves with all changes in our life is the biggest art of living.

***

WATER & BLOOD

*Our body is full of water but whenever it hurts, blood comes out. And our heart is full of blood but whenever it hurts, tears (water) come out.

***

Thank you Lord

"Thank you Lord, for giving me the ability to share this message and for giving me so many wonderful people with whom to share it."

If you have read this far, and are thankful for all that you have been blessed with, how can you not send it on?

I thank God for everything.

***

THINK GOOD, DO GOOD & BE GOOD

Tough times are like physical exercise, you may not like it while you are doing it but tomorrow you will be stronger because of it. Whenever we do something positive in life even if no one is watching, we rise a little bit in our own eyes. Think good, be good, do good.

***

MEDICAL & MORAL SCIENCE

Medical science says, an injury on a tongue heals the quickest. Moral Science says, an injury caused by a tongue takes the longest time to heal.

***

TRAFFIC SIGNAL

A valuable lesson that a traffic signal teaches us: every problem is like a red signal, if we wait for some time, it will turn green. You are never as good as everyone tells you when you win, and you are never as bad as they say when you lose.

***

HAPPINESS

Happiness cannot be traveled to, owned, earned or won. It is the spiritual experience of living every minute with love, grace and gratitude.

Always tell your problems to 1% people who genuinely love you because 50% people don't care of your problems and 49% people become happy when you are in a problem. A hard but true fact.

Brief Profile of Dr. A.S. Vishnu Bharath

PRESENT

- Practicing Sr. Chartered Accountant from past 40 years
- Vice President of APS Education Trust, Bangalore.
- Chairman – PHF Co., (P) Ltd-Transit Living Service Apartments
- Executive President – Karnataka Federation of United Nations UNESCO
- Director – CANFINA Financial Services, Subsidiary of Canara Bank.

- Chairman – NMKRV Degree College.
- President – Vasavi Vedha Nidhi Trust, Sancrit school.
- President- Paraspara Charitable Trust.
- Trustee – Welfare Trust of GMR Infra.
- Trustee – RSS Trust, RV Institutions, Bangalore
- Member – Tax Advisory Committee of Southern India
- Member – Fiscal Laws Committee (FICCI), New Delhi
- Donor-Trustee – Vasavi Sarada Ladies Hostel
- Secretary – SLAS Charitable Trust.
- President – Karnataka Service Apartments Providers Association.

PAST

- Chairman – Southern India Regional Council of Institute of Chartered Accountants of India. Recipient of Best Region award of ICAI
- President – Karnataka State Chartered Accountants Association
- Chairman – Bangalore Branch of SIRC of ICAI. Received
- Best Branch award of ICAI.
- President – Vasavi CA Charitable Trust.
- Managing Committee member of FKCCI for 18 years.

AWARDS

- HONORABLE DOCTRATE for Social Service and contribution to Society received from Mangalore University.
- HONORARY PROFESSORSHIP for Communication skills by Tumkur University.
- RASHTREEYA UDYOG Award from International Economic Forum
- VIKAS JYOTHI Award from All India National Unity Organisation
- VASAVI SIRI Award from Vysya Community Association
- KANNADA SIRI from Kannada Sahithya Parishath

AUTHORED

- PERSONAL GUIDE TO INCOME TAX Published by FKCCI.
- A WOMANS WORLD – Released by Governor of Karnataka.
- A MAN'S WORLD – All about how to achieve success
- KNOW MORE – Knowledge is Strength
- ARYA VYSYA BOOK- All about Arya Vysya's
- "HEALTH IS WEALTH AND IT IS TAX FREE" Tips for good health.
- "LIFE IS PRECIOUS" Importance of Human life.
- "BANK UPON YOUR BANK" Released by FKCCI.

- "VARIETY IS SPICE IN LIFE" Short stories.
- "FESTIVALS OF INDIA" All about Indian Festivals.
- "I LOVE MY INDIA" Sponsored by Canara Bank.
- "Words of Wisdom" Sponsored by ITC Ltd.,
- "Failure is stepping stone for success" spon by GMR Infra Ltd.,
- "Life, Friendship & Happiness" sponsored by GMR Infra Ltd.,
- "Adinarayana Mahime" of SLAS Charitable Trust.
- " V CAT Referencer" A guide for Business man.
- " God The Almighty"
- "Life is like a journye on a train"
- "Centurian Narmadabai Ananthachar"

OTHERS

- Toured all over the world & Member of Red Cross Society
- Given Interview in AIR and Doordarshan – Public Cause
- Has keen interest in Farming and Agriculture
- Good Sportsman and Regular Swimmer & Yoga enthusiast

Phone Nos.41324734/35, 40927835,
Mobile: 98807 01701

Email: vishnubharathco@gmail.
com, info@vbandco.com
Web: vishnubharath.com

If you like this book, pass it on to your
friends, relatives and well wishers.
If you have any comments please send it to my mail.
vishnubharathco@gmail.com

Cover Page Baby: Adhyanth S.
Inside Pages Image Courtesy : http://www.pixabay.com/